T0196414

Out of the Abundance of the Heart

ASHLEY JUNE SMITH

authorHOUSE®

AuthorHouse™
1663 Liberty Drive
Bloomington, IN 47403
www.authorhouse.com
Phone: 1-800-839-8640

Published by AuthorHouse 3/9/2012

ISBN: 978-1-4685-5797-8 (e)
ISBN: 978-1-4685-5798-5 (sc)

Library of Congress Control Number: 2012903732

TABLE OF CONTENTS

THE WORD (IN SPOKEN WORD)

A MESSAGE FOR BELIEVERS

POETIC MUSINGS

ON A PERSONAL NOTE

SECTION ONE:
THE WORD (IN SPOKEN WORD)

The Word became flesh and made his dwelling among us. We have seen his glory, the glory of the one and only Son, who came from the Father, full of grace and truth.

-JOHN 1:14

REFLECTIONS ON JOHN 1

In the beginning
Was the Word
And the Word was
With God
And the Word
Was God
He was
With God in the beginning
So, truth be told,
There's nothing new under the sun
Yet all things are made new
Under His Son
The key to life, He is the light
That shines in the dark places
Of our hearts, minds, and souls
Making known the unknown
He turns over every stone
It's like 100 watts in every crack and crevice,
Without exception
Freeing us from deception and our misperceptions
I'm talkin' about a
Light SO BRIGHT that darkness can't overcome it
John tried to explain it, but most people shunned it
And though through Him the world was made,
They just couldn't understand
That Jesus wasn't just another nice dude,
Or an ordinary man.

The Word became flesh and set up residence
And to all who received Him,
He gave the right to be a resident
Of the Kingdom of God, a child of the Most High
This is the One about whom John tried to testify
The One full of grace and truth,
So holy John wasn't worthy to untie His shoes
And even though no one has seen the Father,
He was made known through His Son
So, don't get it twisted,
John wasn't the Messiah or a prophet
But the voice of one
Calling in the wilderness
To prepare the way for the Lord
The Holy Lamb of God
Who came to take away the sins of the world
And this was God's plan from the very beginning
Because
In the beginning
Was the Word
And the Word was
With God
And the Word
Was God
He was
With God in the beginning,
Then
    The Word
        Became
           Flesh.

REFLECTIONS ON JOHN 2

Although His hour had not yet come
Turning water to wine
Is the first of the signs
To reveal the glory of the Son
As He secretly takes away
The shame of the bridegroom
His authority is assumed
Yet His momma and the servants
Are among the select few
Who witness this miracle
And can give credit where credit is due
Then the scene shifts,
And now Jesus is consumed
With zeal for His Father's house,
So He quickly clears the room
He's flippin' tables in the temple
Righteous indignation at the men who
Disregard the foreigner and the widow
By committing acts that are sinful
So Jesus brings justice and salvation
By opening the temple to all nations
Tearing down empty structures
Devoid of the kabod Yahweh
Declaring that it will be rebuilt,
All on the third day
He points to the resurrection
As His authority is questioned
And although confused at the time
The disciples later press rewind
And recall the Holy Scripture

Now seeing a fuller picture
Of the Godhead three in one
And how the glory of the Father
Has been revealed through the Son.

REFLECTIONS ON JOHN 3

There's more to be seen
In John 3 than just verse 16.
We know God so loved the world
That He sent His Son
But also darkness tries to hide
Because the light has come.
Not to condemn, but expose sin
And bring life eternal
As we lift up the Son of Man
Because He's the only one who
Brings salvation and truth to all of humanity
Letting us know that entrance into the Kingdom
Requires that we be
Born again, not of the flesh,
But of the Spirit
Telling us about a God
Who gives the Spirit without limit
And John was sent ahead
To prepare us to hear it
As a friend of the bridegroom
He waited and listened
And with the Messiah's arrival
John's joy was made complete
Declaring, "He must become greater,
And I must decrease."

Come, see a man who told me everything I ever did. Could this be the Messiah?

-John 4:29

My Testimony

Tell me,
How do You write Your words
On the walls of a heart that's been
Chopped and screwed so many times
That mere rhymes and smooth lines
Can't erase the pain?
And they say,
Your Son came
On Calvary was slain
Gave sight to the blind and
Swag to the lame
But sometimes I wonder
If He even knows my name?

But then it's like
I'm the woman at the well
Tryin' to hide, but He rips the veil
And proceeds to tell
My whole life story
Says He has somethin' for me
Livin' water to quench my thirst
Straight real talk
It's not rehearsed
Inviting me to worship in Spirit and Truth
Got me lookin' like, "Man, who *is* this dude?!"
Could it be the Messiah
Callin' me higher
Release from guilt and shame

Up from the muck and the mire?

And now I've got a testimony
Designed to inspire
Others to come and see
The man who heals broken hearts
And sets captives free
'Cause He's the Savior of the world
And now you'll believe
'Cause you'll find if you seek
And He'll do for you
What He did for me.

I wait for the Lord more than watchmen wait for the morning, more than watchmen wait for the morning.

-PSALM 130:6

I WAIT

Lord,
I wait for You
More than watchmen
Wait for the morning
When darkness is at its darkest
And sin overcomes me
Out of the depths
My voice cries to You
Longing for Your mercy
With all that is within me
I wait.

In Your Word I put my hope
For Your Word is a sure foundation
As sure as the rising of the sun
And with the rising of Your Son
There is redemption.
With You there is forgiveness
We can serve You with reverence
And because each day
Your mercies are new
More than watchmen
Wait for the morning
I choose
To wait
For You.

Silver or gold I do not have, but what I do have I give you. In the name of Jesus Christ of Nazareth, walk.

REFLECTIONS ON ACTS 3

They thought they knew, but they had no idea
Moses tried to explain it,
But they still couldn't see Him
So they killed the Author of Life,
But death didn't defeat Him
And there's no other name
By which men are saved ·
'Cause God raised Him from the dead
Now it's time to change our ways
'Cause He's more than just a carpenter,
He's our Savior and King
He's the liberator too, so let freedom ring
In every classroom and dorm room,
The caf and the quad
We've been empowered and sent
As ambassadors for God
To bring a message of healing and hope
For the lame and the blind
That faith in Jesus' name will work every time
Faith in His name alone
Is where our wholeness is found
No longer held captive, and no longer bound
We've been freed for a purpose
Time to stop sittin' down
Jesus saved us from destruction
Set our feet on solid ground
He's the King of Glory
At His feet we gladly cast our crowns

Crying Holy, Holy, Holy
Is the Lord God Almighty
Who was, and is, and is to come
The risen King, God's only Son
He conquered death and the grave
Our God is mighty to save
We've been sent on a mission
Like Peter we boldly proclaim
The things we've seen and heard
The reason why He came
We've been transformed
To live our lives as agents of change
So, I don't have much money,
But what I do have I give
By the power of Jesus' name
Stand up and live.

Therefore I tell you, do not worry about your life, what you will eat or drink; or about your body, what you will wear. Is not life more than food, and the body more than clothes?... But seek first his kingdom and his righteousness, and all these things will be given to you as well.

-MATTHEW 6:25,33

SERMON ON THE MOUNT

Jesus, I need You
To lead me and guide me
And stay right beside me
As I try to deal with the feelings
Deep down inside me.
I can't see through the darkness
Yet am afraid of Your light.
The reality is, it hurts
When the light gets too bright.
I feel like the weight of the world
Is on my shoulders,
And I can't muster up the faith
It takes to move boulders.

My heart breaks
For the prostitute, the destitute,
The crack addict who don't know the Truth,
The alcoholic, the neglected youth,
The prisoner, even for the homeless dude.

Everybody on the block's got a story to tell,
So put names to the faces,
'Cause sometimes we fail
To realize and fully recognize
The truth covered up by the lies

We tell ourselves,
Just so we don't have to look into people's eyes.
Just 'cause we don't acknowledge the humanity
In the people they were created to be,
Don't mean they ain't constantly
Strugglin' to be free.

We always talkin' 'bout the love of Jesus,
But stead'ly doin' only that which pleases us,
Not bein' sensitive to the real needs
Of those around us.
And I ain't tryin' to make it sound like
I'm the perfect Christian,
'Cause believe,
You ain't gotta dig too deep
To expose my own sin.
But I do feel the need
To vent my anger and frustration
With the current situation,
How we seem to drift
Deeper into religion
And further from relation.

I ain't claimin' to have all the answers,
I don't know how to make things right,
But as hard as it is, I'm willing to fight.
Tryin' to put my faith in Christ and not my sight.
Wrestlin' to understand Matthew 6:25-33,
When I still see the homeless man's daily reality.

And even though the pressure
Builds up inside of me,
I'm prayin' to know God more,
Not necessarily for relief.

But it's only in God's strength
That I can persevere,
Recognizin' that my doubt, pain, and fear
Are incredibly sincere.
And, I'll admit that I was afraid to face it,
But ignorin' it don't erase it
So I lay it on the altar,
And refuse to be complacent.

Therefore, if anyone is in Christ, the new creation has come:
The old has gone, the new is here!

-2 Corinthians 5:17

REDEEMED

I lift my head up to the sky and cry
That I have been redeemed.
Wondering how a Holy God could make clean
That which was unfit to even be seen.
I don't understand it, but He planned it.
He wrote the script, the story of a King.
The One who came down from the heavenlies
To declare His love for you and me.
See, He became flesh, took on sin and death
So that I could stand before you
Declaring that I'm a mess and not distress
Because I'm covered
By His blood and righteousness.
So even though like Paul I cry,
"O, wretched man am I",
There's hope knowing that Christ paid the price
So that we may live and not die.
39 lashes, 3 nails, 1 cross
Jesus gave His life to seek and save the lost.
Therefore, rejoice with me
As we witness the transformation
Behold, the old man has passed away,
We've become a new creation.
No longer bound by guilt and shame
No longer tainted 'cause He erased the stains,

And although at times we may wonder
What it all means
We can lift our heads up to the sky and cry
That we have been redeemed!

But he was pierced for our transgressions, he was crushed for our iniquities; the punishment that brought us peace was on him, and by his wounds we are healed.

-ISAIAH 53:5

THE CROSS

People don't really understand
The price that He paid.
As kids we are told cute lil' stories
That come pre-packaged, ready-made.
We hear about His hands
With the scars and the nails.
Romanticized images of Christ the Savior
—never fails.
I remember hearin' preachers say a few words
About the death, burial, and resurrection.
The congregation claps, the choir sings a selection.
They made it sound like it was easy,
Like Jesus died in His sleep.
How many people can imagine
Having rusty nails driven through their feet?
If they only knew what really took place.
We don't often hear
About how they spit in His face.
They don't talk about the army of men,
Who nearly beat Him to death,
Or how they mocked Him
Even as He took His last breath.
Did you know about the crown
Of needlelike thorns?
Or about the sword in His side,
How His flesh was torn?
He hung for hours in excruciating pain.

You can't tell me that my Jesus died in vain!

I see a lot of people
Wear a cross around their neck.
Askin' myself if they need a reality check?
Do they understand that Jesus' death
Was a form of payment
For every sin committed,
Or do they wear it
Just to make a fashion statement?
There's power in having a revelation
Of what the Cross really means.
God opens the eyes of the heart
To show you what the natural eye hasn't seen.
For those of you who haven't been saved,
You need to act quick
'Cause these are truly the last days.
All it takes is a heartfelt confession
A genuine belief in the death,
Burial, and resurrection.
For those who have heard the story
Over a million times,
Let me break it down even more
In the rest of this rhyme.
John 3:16…*For God so loved the world…*
You already know the rest.
God sent His only Son,
So we need to give Him our best.
It's not really askin' very much
If you take the time to review.
Think about how Jesus suffered,
All He went through just for you.
I'm not excluding myself.
I don't want your view to be slanted.

God's been dealin' with me
About takin' His love for granted.
I was just like everybody else,
I heard about what happened on Calvary.
But God changed my heart,
And made it come to life inside of me.
I see it for what it truly is,
No longer just a Sunday school story, or a fairytale
The ultimate manifestation of love,
Jesus gave His life
So we wouldn't have to burn in hell.
So, if nothin' else, please understand
There's A LOT more to the Cross,
Than the nails in His hand.

SECTION TWO:
A Message for Believers

*Do not judge, or you too will be judged. For in the same way
you judge others, you will be judged, and with the measure
you use, it will be measured to you.*

-MATTHEW 7:1-2

CHURCH AS USUAL?

If people ask me, "What is your religion?",
And I don't say that I'm a Christian
They may look at me and think "hypocrite",
Since I talk about Christ
In most of the rhymes I spit.
But everything done in the name of "Christianity"
Ain't that nice, so I let 'em know:
I'm not bound by "religion",
But I *am* a follower of Christ.

WWJD…what *would* Jesus do?
Well, for one thing,
He'd get up off of the pew,
And lay aside the self-righteous,
"holier than thou" attitude.

Jesus would show love
To the dudes that be poppin' clips,
And He'd minister to prostitutes and pimps,
And alcoholics, and addicts,
And the dudes that be chiefin',
And liars, and prisoners, and er'body
That be creepin' and freakin'.

And if you wanna be extra *extra* real with it,
Jesus wouldn't be bombin' abortion clinics.
And you may not believe it or know it,

But Jesus was *not* a homophobic.
I ain't tryin' to say that He would've condoned it,
But all this hatin' in the name of the Church,
Ain't doin' nothin' but makin' things worse.
We need to grow up
And come to the realization
That this walk is about love
And not condemnation.
Take it back to the basics,
Let's start at the foundation.
Hate don't cause folks to accept salvation.

What would it look like
For the Church to do as it should
Instead of gossipin' in the sanctuary,
While dudes are dyin' in the hood?
Where are our priorities?
Are they really where they ought to be?
Jesus came to heal the broken-hearted,
And set the captives free,
But we're stead'ly puttin' people in bondage
To man-made rules and religiosity.

The Holy Spirit convicts,
Ain't nobody perfect.
We're called to speak the truth in love,
Not deliver a verdict.
So, just plant the seed
So it can be watered and grow,
But please believe
That you reap what you sow.

These people honor me with their lips, but their hearts are far from me.

-MATTHEW 15:8

REVOLUTION

It's time for a revolution.
I'm tired of this dilution.
Mixin' two parts world with one part God
Is a poisonous solution.
Watered down Christianity, in need of revival.
Speak life to these dry bones,
It's vital to our survival.

It's time out for bein' a C-M-E church member.
God is real *every*day
Not just Christmas, Mother's Day, and Easter.
He has a work for us to do,
So polish up the armor.
Please open your eyes,
'Cause judgment is right around the corner.

Grow up, get off the milk,
Partake of the meat of God's Word.
We've been commissioned
To share the Good News
With those who've never heard,
But how can we expect to spread the Gospel
When we don't even live how Jesus said?
James 2:20 lets us know that,
"Faith without works is dead."
Tell me how you can go from creepin'
And gettin' blazed on Saturday night,
To standin' up in the *pulpit*

Talkin' 'bout how Jesus
Is *the way, the truth, and the life?*

It breaks my heart to see
All the hypocrisy in the Church.
The House of God should be a place of healin',
Yet more and more people are gettin' hurt.
The pews are full of falsely pious Pharisees
Who won't take the time to see
That we're turnin' away an entire generation
With all the gossip and religiosity.
Stop trippin' off of whether
Girls are wearin' skirts or jeans,
And focus on if they've gotten on their knees,
To accept Jesus as their Lord and King.

It's not about man-made rules and regulations.
It's time for the saints of God to be real with it
All across the nation,
'Cause even after all the shoutin', the hallelujahs,
And gettin' slain in the Spirit,
God is still sayin', "they honor me with their lips
But in their hearts they don't feel it."

We go to church on Sunday mornings
Dressed up from our head down to our feet.
Thinkin' we're too good
To break out of the four walls
And help the brothers and sisters on the street.
When nothin' we did in and of ourselves
Could've gotten us where we are,
Had it not been for the grace of God
Which has carried us this far.
So we shouldn't think so highly of ourselves

That we can't be a blessing to others,
'Cause our *righteousness is as filthy rags*
Had it not been for the blood of Jesus as our cover.

Well, now that I've spoken to the Body,
Let me holla at those on the outside lookin' in.
True, there are a lot of things wrong
With the Church today,
But that's no excuse for *you* to sin.

And for those who have prayin' mommas,
And think that maybe you'll just wait,
You may be young, but know,
You can't get to heaven on your momma's faith.

And when judgment day comes,
And it's time to stand before the Throne,
He ain't gon' ask you how the church folk lived,
'Cause you'll be standin' all alone.
One of the choir members may have lied on you,
And you ain't been back ever since,
I'm not sayin' that their behavior is justified,
But it won't hold up in *your* defense.
You're not promised tomorrow,
So you need to get to know Jesus for yourself,
'Cause when it's all said and done,
It ain't about nobody else.
He wants nothin' more
Than to form a relationship with you today.
I beg you to look at Romans 10:9,
Confess and believe, 'cause it's the only way.

How good and pleasant it is when God's people live together in unity!

-PSALM 133:1

TRUE COMMUNITY

We talk about community,
So let unity come
Yet it's easier said than done
When hearts have been broken
And we constantly run
From each other and from the One
Who loves us so much He sent His Son.

I don't know your story,
And I doubt you know mine,
But ain't it about time
We left the masquerade behind?
'Cause I'm tired of pretendin'
That when I became a Christian I stopped sinnin'
Life is too short,
And we don't know what we missin'
When we try to hide our mess
Behind religious activity
While the God of heaven invites us to be free
'Cause bein' broken ain't bad
It's just reality
And band-aid solutions
Never heal our wounds properly.
So I'ma commit to bein' real with you
And the God who made me
'Cause only then will we begin
To experience true community

Free from guilt and shame
Secure in the love of our Creator
With all our sin exposed
Covered by the blood of our Savior
We take our place amongst the imperfect saints
Trustin' only in His perfect grace
A community of believers,
Lettin' His Spirit lead us,
Convict us, and teach us,
Bound together in love,
The enemy can't defeat us,
So let's take a stand and make a decision,
A true testament that we serve
The One who is risen
By choosing to live in unity,
Not in division.

But you will receive power when the Holy Spirit comes on
you; and you will be my witnesses in Jerusalem, and in all
Judea and Samaria, and to the ends of the earth.

-ACTS 1:8

(W)HOL(L)Y DISCONTENT

The revolution
       The revolution
             The revolution will
Not be televised
It will be live
As we live our faith out loud
In surround sound and high definition
Divinely re-mastered proposition
No more street corner proclamations
Drive-by salvations
A new declaration of independence
…be free…

Freedom from religion
Freedom of relation
Let go of the status quo
'Cause life ain't black and white
And the Gospel ain't grey

Experience the fullness of God's love and grace
Admitting that we are perfect(ly) weak
Turn up the volume and watch the Lord speak
…red-letter edition…

Changing our realities from present to preferred
Souls awakened, hearts stirred
Faith reacting with the Spirit's power

(W)hol(l)y discontent
Now is the time. This very hour.

Change agents rooted and grounded
Surrounded by the great cloud
Layin' aside sins and weights
As we run this race
We must endure.

We must no longer confuse
Apologetics with apologies
It is for freedom He set us free
Therefore, I DE-CLARE WAR
On strongholds and principalities
Sendin' demons to the infirmary
So, let the battle begin
As one Body in Christ
The Alpha and Omega
Beginning and end.

Lord, pour out Your Spirit on all men
That Your sons and daughters may prophesy
Refusing to compromise or apologize
For their visions and dreams

For, this is the generation of them
That will seek Your face
Cling to the Truth
Satan's lies erased
Start fresh.
Clean slate.
Called to be enemies of the state
Of confusion.

We've been appointed and commissioned
Sent out to be a witness
So, let the light of Christ shine bright
In *our* Jerusalems day and night

Lord, please empower and shape us
We'll go where You take us
Worthless idols denied
Grabbing hold of You and You alone…
Christ Crucified.

SECTION THREE:
POETIC MUSINGS

WEIGHTS AND MEASURES

How much does a poem weigh?
Can its lines be measured
In impassioned heartbeats,
As irregular rhythms cause phrases to *speed up*
Or draaaaaaaa aaaaag,
Or calmly flow along?

Is white space the equivalent of held breath?

Built up pressure causing you to let it all out in a
        sudden burst of panicked release.
Gasping
        for
            air
With each word that fills the page.
Finally, feeling the burdens lifting,
As your innermost thoughts
Are delicately placed
On the scales of perception
Waiting to be judged by all.

SIMPLICITY IN A COMPLEX WORLD

Red, White, and Blue…
The colors of
Flashing lights as
5-0 invades the American ghetto.
Rushin' to the spot where ol' boy got shot
Or to the cut-rate on Baucum Ave.
Where urban businessmen make frequent
        transactions
                interactions
                        satisfaction
As supplies run low and pockets get fat.
The trick on the corner gets molested,
Handcuffed, and arrested.

Pit bulls and strays bark and break free
As gun shots ring out
Everybody drops and takes cover
Tryin' to recover from the trauma that *is* life.

I can hear the news reporters now…
"Oh, by the way, there was another drive-by last
        night…"
A few people were hit, some were killed…
You know, same ol' same ol'.

No one notices the little boy
Playing in the vacant lot
That the neighborhood kids call a park.
Chasin' fire flies and imaginin' steamboats
And elephants in the sky.
The epitome of innocence.
The sirens don't faze him.

As he goes to buy 25 cents worth
Of penny candy from King's.
All that matters in this moment
Is his sweet reward.
He doesn't care that the store
Is on the very same corner
Where hustlas are shootin' craps
And ol' school playas are sippin' gin.
It doesn't faze him.
Life, for him, right now, is
sweet
and
simple.

MISSED COMMUNICATION

I asked you an unheard question
Words passed directly from my soul to yours
Without risk of being lost in translation.
Flowing like gentle breezes,
The soft crackle of winter fires,
Or the echo of ocean waters
Coming through abandoned seashells.

Yet instead of feeling close to you,
I feel the emptiness of that last echo
Reverberating off the walls of my heart.
Then I wonder if we speak different languages,
Because intimacy has been replaced
With ambiguity.

As I feel us drifting apart,
The volume of those unheard questions
Slowly begins to be turned up
So that our miscommunication
Doesn't become missed communication.
As our chances of being close yet again
Pass by
Because I was afraid
To speak up.

INSIDE OUT

Cracks of light
Seep through vertical slits
As the all-too-familiar
CLA-CLINK resounds and
I sit.
Waiting.

I used to use my pencil to help me cope
So, I wrote, and wrote, and…
Maybe they got lost in the mail.

Here, each minute is like an hour
Each hour, a day
Each day…
…it doesn't matter
Because that day is still
So far away.

Your world doesn't move as slowly as mine.
You're too busy to feel
Yourself inhale and exhale.
You're winding your rubber band too tight.

At least here I have time
So much time.
(I am free) to breathe
Stale, mold-laden air.
And think
Inventing new reasons
I haven't heard from you.

You still care about me
Don't you?

Do you realize how much you mean to me?
I guess my actions spoke louder than my words.

I am sorry I left when you were so young.
I wanted to be there
…but I couldn't.

I know I missed watching you grow up.
I thought about you all the time.
…still do.

I can't undo the past.
I would if I could.

I want to be there now, but
I need you to meet me
halfway.

IN HIS IMAGE

God created you in His own image
He created your mind to seek wisdom and truth
He created your hands to build up, not tear down
He created your arms to embrace, not push away
He created your heart to love,
Not only Him,
But yourself and others
He created your eyes to see,
Not only the physical,
But also what lies deep within
He created your ears to listen
To the words of others,
But also to that which goes unsaid

God created you in His own image
You are not weak,
But are strong because of Him
You are not poor,
But are rich in the love that only He gives
You are not lazy,
But are hardworking
Because He is a God of excellence
You are not ignorant,
But are intelligent beyond measure
Because of His wisdom
You are a strong, Black man
Created in the image of God Himself.

WORTH THE WAIT

Our souls connect
Becoming one
Allowing you to love me
Loving you unselfishly
I can't describe it
I already love you
From deep within myself
Wanting you to know
That I'm here for you
To support and encourage you
It's O.K. to cry sometimes
I know how strong you are
You don't have to prove your manhood
Mighty man of valor
Walking in integrity
Saving
    waiting
        worth it
Just for you.

I want to be your partner
Your helpmeet
I will make our house a home
I will follow you
As you follow Christ
I am waiting for you
Because not just anyone will do.

WELCOME TO MY WORLD

In poetry I find my release
A love affair on loose leaf
Passionate words in between the sheets
Transcending space and time with each rhyme
As pen and paper meet
It's the mystery of creation
Divine inspiration
Beyond infatuation
I'm fallin' in love with each word,
Beautiful phrase, noun and verb
A heavenly melody to relieve the stress
A temporary escape, no need to impress
I'm in my own world and my mind is free
Flowin' with the rhythm
Comin' alive with the beat
Playin' complicated, syncopated notes with my ink
A four-part (dis)harmony that's makin' me think
About romance and laughter
And not-so-happily-ever-afters
It's a never-ending symphony
A dichotomous soliloquy
As my pen becomes the key
To release my heart from its captivity
Thoughts no longer bound
Behind the blue bars of these pages
Creativity leaking through,
Leaving its mark on these white spaces
Broad strokes and fine lines
Unapologetic in my tone and rhyme
The authenticity won't cease
'Cause it's in poetry
That I find
My release.

MIDDLE PASSAGE

I want to write a poem
That reaches beyond intellect
To the place where soul and mind intersect,
That bridges the past and the present
And causes people to reconnect.

I want to write a poem
That gives honor where honor is due
To Angelou, Giovanni, Williams, Hughes,
Baraka, Washington, Dubois, Garvey
Douglass, Dunbar, Sanchez and Wheatley.

I want to write a poem
That makes people contemplate
What it looks like to come
To the fork in the road and go straight,
That challenges the norms of society,
But questions popular non-conformity.

I want to write a poem
That incites a revolution
And discusses the evolution
Of oral history
By analyzing Negro spirituals,
Modern-day minstrels,
And everything in between.

I want to write a poem
About the Crucifixion,
Personal conviction
And the difference between
Spirituality and organized religion.

I want to write a poem
About church-folk and sinners,
Drug addicts and prisoners,
About knowing when to fight back,
And when to surrender.

I want to write a poem
That is a stream of (social) consciousness.
A continuous flow that's not afraid to digress,
Nevertheless making progress towards
Raising personal awareness.

One day,
I will write a poem.

SPOKEN (LIKE A TRUE POET)

My pencil is mightier than a sword
So, I write the wrongs of the past
Trying to account for the mass
Destruction of culture and creativity,
Recognizing this modern-day slavery,
Mistaken identity.
I go back
And erase stray marks
Pressing in to bubble in
The circles completely.

This *is* my standardized (w)rite of passage.

I simply cannot, will not, will *rot*
If I hold back any longer.

I will RAISE MY VOICE, and not apologize
Refusing to believe the lies
I tell myself about what poetry is,
Because I realize
that this 8 ½ by 11 mirror
Reflects *my* style.

I will no longer imitate or
Regurgitate, that to which I cannot relate,
Or feel that I have no place
In the intellectual marketplace
Simply because my verses are
Best delivered vocally.

I am tired of trying
To convince myself

Of this legitimacy.
I mean, which came first,
Written
Or oral history?

So, from this point on,
I
must
SPEAK.

MY SOUL LOOKS BACK

Lift every voice and sing
The forgotten songs of our ancestors
About undying strength,
And the will to overcome.

It is an oral history
That tells the pain of our Fathers
And the suffering of our Mothers.

The ultimate struggle for freedom.

Times have changed,
Yet the dream is still deferred.

We are anything but free
As we continue to believe
That the word *nigga* can be reclaimed.
Or that *trick* and *hoe* are acceptable
Substitutes for *lover* and *friend*.

As we look at the present in light of our past
Maybe we can finally answer Hughes' inquiry.
Because we see the heavy load
Caused by treating each other as enemies.

Let's not wait for everything to explode.

Precious Memories

I remember when we would get all dressed up for church,
ruffles from head to toe, only to fall asleep on the pew
behind the organ halfway through the sermon.

I remember when the highlight of the week was riding
with Granny to the grocery store. She always knew how to
make the simplest errand seem like the greatest adventure.

I remember when I was restricted to riding my bike up
and down the street in front of the house, and the freedom
I felt when I was finally permitted to go within a two-
block radius.

I remember when the streetlights coming on was the
indication that I needed to make my way home, or risk
being called out in front of all my friends as Granny yelled
for me through the screen door.

I remember when squirming around in the chair as I was
getting my hair done would warrant a tap on the knuckles
with the comb.

I remember when after walking that block and a half back
from church on Sunday afternoons, we were met with
the overwhelming aroma of a homemade meal fit for the
Pastor.

I remember when we would play in the water from
the garden hose because there was no pool in the
neighborhood to offer relief from the summer's heat.

I remember when we could walk to the corner store on Monday and get enough penny candy to last until after next Sunday's service for only 50 cents.

I remember when us playing double-dutch was determined by whether or not Granny would let us use her clothesline after everything was dry.

I remember when we'd hang a curtain in between the kitchen and the bedroom because we lived in a two bedroom shotgun with no doors to separate rooms.

One day I realized that kids grow up, loved ones pass on, and houses get torn down...

...but memories this deep never fade away.

A Piece of My Passion

From deep within my mind
I'm working overtime
To translate emotions
Into catchy phrases
And lines that rhyme
Using my pen
Like Michelangelo used paintbrushes
These pages are my Sistine Chapel

Yet, I can never be more creative
Than my Creator
I'm talkin' similes and metaphors
Heaven's heights, the oceans' floors
The original spoken word artist
He spoke the Word and
It *was*
'Cause He's the Author and the Finisher
Divine soul-replenisher
Living water, thirst quencher
Saw my sin and went to
Calvary just to save a wretch like me.

I'm sayin, how could I not worship
The One who conquered death and the grave?
Made me whole, broke my chains
Calls me a daughter, not a slave
Prepared a table before me
In the very presence of my enemies
Gave me righteousness as a gift
Grace for when I slip
Anointed me for His service
And put His words on my lips

So as I put my pen to this paper
And let these words overflow
Please know that the gift
Is never greater than the Gift Giver
So I'll gladly take my place
As a broken vessel willing to be used
And I'll give honor where honor is due
And as I focus my attention on Elohim
I pray that through these words, people can see
That the only life worth living
Is one surrendered to Him
Learning to seek His glory,
Not the adoration of men

So with each stroke of my pen
I'll continue to give Him praise
And offer all that I am
To the Ancient of Days.

SECTION FOUR:
ON A PERSONAL NOTE

Out of the Abundance of the Heart

I put my pencil to the paper
And let these words overflow
Cascading down the page like Niagara
Falls – one
              thought
                  to the
                       next
Sometimes reaching outside of myself
And losing all context.

I reload my No.2 in order to find release
To be set free from (self-inflicted?) bondage
Urging my captive thoughts to follow
The drinking gourd and Harriet
Up before I am too afraid to move
Foreword to this underground rail
Road trip to divine revelation

I attempt to write the wrongs of my mind
Trying to account for why I feel like I can't cry
But must hold it all inside and hide
From what's real

I've got these steel bars around my heart
Don't really know how or where to start
But I'll keep writing
Hoping
That my words will somehow set me free
For out of the abundance of the heart
The mouth speaks
And even though I have a little of everything and
A whole lot of nothing to say…

Let's talk…
About how I continue to let lies overshadow Truth
Or how when I take a step forward
I seem to move back two
How just like Paul
I do the very thing I hate to do

Let's talk about how
God feels distant and everyone else disinterested
…and maybe they should be…
Because my problems seem small
When you *really* think of it

Let's talk about how
My heart longs to know the father I never knew
And even though my mother did all she could do
I still want to be *daddy's* little girl

Let's talk about how
I desire to reconnect with my history
To know the family that God chose for me
The one that hid from me

Let's talk about how
I'm tired of pretending that everything is O.K.
This stained-glass masquerade
Too afraid to look past
The pretty colored haze
And focus on the
Individual.
Broken.
Pieces.

Let's talk about how
I'm 22 years old and a liar
Hiding behind 'I don't know's
Because I'm 20 years too old for a pacifier

Let's talk…
About how talk is cheap
(at least that's what they tell me)
Because even if I keep talking I'll still be
Unable to change history and unsure
Of how to proceed to be truly set free
I'm really struggling to believe
That opening up is better
Than shutting down completely

Let's talk about how
I don't know what's real anymore
How I long to be four
Before life got complicated

Let's talk about how
My pencil is running out of lead
And I'm running out of patience
But I need to finish this and try to make sense
Of my stream of consciousness

…because I like closure…

So maybe I'll just
Eat a cookie (or two, or three…)
And go to bed
Praying that the thoughts that fill my head
Will be carried away in my dreams
And I'll realize that nothing is as it seems

Because when I close my eyes
I create my *own* reality

But the reality is I must choose
Will I be content with whole lies and half-truths?
Like when Saul became Paul
I want these scales to fall
So I can see clearly
Not only what *has* been
But what *will* be
I don't want to walk around blindly

So, I'll let go of this anger and stop fighting
Change my fist to an open hand
So the Lord can guide me
And I'll try not to always keep my thoughts
Under lock and key
Because I know
That out of the abundance of the heart
The mouth speaks.

A PRAYER TO MY GOD

As I sit here and think of You,
There's only one thing that I can do.
I praise You for how good You've been to me
I'm no longer afraid of fulfillin' my destiny.
The purpose You've called me for
Will not be forsaken.
The passion You've placed in my heart
Will not be shaken.

I love You with all of my mind and my soul,
My heart I place in Your hands for You to hold.
Because I know You will protect me
From dangers seen and unseen,
And by Your Son's blood
I have been redeemed.

If I had ten thousand tongues
It wouldn't be sufficient.
I put my trust in a God
Who's omnipotent, omnipresent, and omniscient.
Jehovah Jireh, my provider.
Jehovah Rapha, my healer.
My righteousness is found in Jehovah-Tsidkenu.
El Shaddai, all of my strength comes from You.

As I pour out my heart before You Lord,
With Faith as my shield,
And the Word as my sword,
I'll go forth and speak the words
You've placed on my lips,
Always seeking Your face,
So that I'll be equipped.

To do the work You've called me to do.
On my knees praying
That I never get ahead of You.
You knew me before I was formed
In my mother's womb
So I'll wait for You,
Just like Peter in the upper room.

You've set me apart,
And appointed me for Your service,
Never again will I believe the enemy
When he says that I'm worthless.
That's a lie from the pit of hell,
And I serve a God of Truth.
You told me to trust in You,
And despise not my youth.
So I ask that You help me
Lead *a life worthy of the call*.
Right now, I put everything aside,
And surrender all.

SOLID GROUND

I look out among the thousands of faces
Searching for one that reminds me of You
I see the familiar eyes of old acquaintances
But that is not enough to ease this feeling.
Lost in the crowd,
All I want is to see Your hand
Reaching out to save me
From the perpetual darkness
That I feel when I am not close to You
I know that if I can find You once more
You can stop my world
From spinning out of control.
When the earthquakes come
To shatter my foundation
It is You alone who can set my feet
On solid ground.

HEART'S CRY

Lord, I believe, but help my unbelief
'Cause my eyes are open, but I just can't see
And my soul cries out within me
As the deep calls unto deep
Wanting to trust in You
Even with tears runnin' down my cheeks

So what do I do
When my sure foundation
Feels so uncertain
And the verses I learned in Sunday school,
Just ain't workin'
And there seem to be
More questions than answers
While doubt spreads like cancer?
I need to know that You're real
That You are my Savior
'Cause I feel like I'm drownin'
And I'm tired of fightin'
And even more sick of cryin'
So that's why I'm writin'

I need Your beauty for my ashes
The oil of joy instead of mournin'
It's kinda dark right now,
But they say joy comes in the mornin'
So, I'ma choose to trust that Your Word is true
That in spite of how I feel,
I can find real hope in You

So just like David in Psalm 103,
I will lift up my head, and boldly decree,
"Bless the Lord, O my soul,
And all that is within me
Bless His holy name"
For both yesterday, and today,
Lord, You are the same
Let me not forget the things You've already done
Like how I've been forgiven and redeemed
By the blood of Your Son
How You planned all the days of my life
Before I lived even one
How Your love is unfailing
And Your power unmatched
How when I strayed from the path,
You stopped to go back
Or how even when I can't feel You,
Your presence is there
How You ultimately bring justice
In a world that's unfair

Even in the times when it's so hard to believe
Or when my vision gets cloudy and it's hard to see
Help me remember
That we walk by faith and not by sight
So I'll trust You over my feelings
And put my faith in Christ.

SPENT

When I see how your heart hurts
It breaks a piece of mine
Knowing that God alone
Can grant me peace of mind
'Cause I can't carry this burden on my shoulders
Feelin' like I'ma break if I try for too much longer
But surrendering all
Isn't nearly as easy as it sounds
Especially when these thoughts
Keep playin' round and round

My soul screams
Yet I cry silent tears
Trying to be a strong woman of faith,
But can't shake these fears
Feeling so helpless,
But wanting to do so much
And still live by the motto,
"In God We Trust"
'Cause that's what a "good Christian"
Is supposed to do
But what happens when the worries are many,
And the prayers are few?

Right now fatigue is setting in,
And on my own I can't stand
Am I left to fall,
Or will He take my hand?
I must choose to believe
That God is still in control
But it's hard to look past circumstances,
If the truth be told

I know that in the end, victory will come
That because of Christ, I've already won
But in anticipation of the future,
I can't deny the present
So I cry out for rest 'cause I'm
Emotionally,
        physically,
                and spiritually
Spent.

Hear my cry, O God; listen to my prayer. From the ends of the earth I call to you, I call as my heart grows faint; lead me to the rock that is higher than I.

-PSALM 61:1-2

LEAD ME TO THE ROCK

I'm on a slippery slope to destruction
In desperate need of a life-line
Wishin' I could press rewind
Turn back the hands of time
To when everything was "just fine"
But I'm livin' in this modern-day Babylon
Captivity of the mind.
Disconnected from the Vine
Vision so cloudy
I can't see the Son shine
And my heart is gettin' as hard
As the broken cisterns I keep turnin' to
Drinking poison instead of Living Water
With each sip forsaking You
For temporary relief that can't quench my thirst
Caught up in a whirlwind
Got me questionin' my worth
Thoughts runnin' through my head so fast
I can't catch my breath
The reality is, I'm not truly livin',
I'm just kinda breathin' to death
Asking where is the hope and the rest?
The solid ground in the midst of the mess?

And suddenly I remember how
You promise to bless
The brokenhearted.

Offering Your strength
After mine has long departed
Peace slipping through my fingers
'Til there's hardly any left,
But instead of giving up,
I'll put Your Word to the test
And choose to trust
That You're bigger than my hang-ups
That instead of complainin',
I should try to lift Your name up
Focusing my attention on You and Your Glory
Believing that in spite of the pain,
You're still writing the story
That in the scope of eternity,
These afflictions are light
That there'll come a day and an hour
When all wrongs are made right
But in the meantime, I can rest in Your love
And stop tryin' to fight

So, Lord, I choose to surrender
Letting You replace this heart of stone
With one that is tender
Please guide me in the path of righteousness
For Your namesake
Breathe new life in me, until I'm fully awake
No longer is it in my own strength that I try
But I'm cryin' out, Lord
Lead me to the Rock
That is higher than I.

Can You Hear Me?

I cry out to God
With everything that is within me
Praying that if nothing else
He'll open my eyes so that I can see
'Cause I want to treat the source
And not just the symptoms
To be an overcomer and not a victim
But does God still move when my faith is weak?
When I don't have the strength to fight
Will He still speak?
I feel like I'm climbing up a mountain
And I'm losing my grip
Trying to stand strong
But I'm about to slip
Afraid I couldn't get back up
If I did happen to fall
Wondering if God still hears me when I call?
I admit I'm in a place of desperation
And maybe it's preparation
But it feels like isolation
And utter separation
I don't know where to go from here
Searching for something to alleviate my fears
Even if the relief is only for an instant
It's better than nothing
When God feels so distant
I'm running out of words
I'm running out of tears
I'm running to my God
Hoping He still hears.

ST. LOUIS

Woman's body is found; police are investigating

The body of a nude woman was discovered about 7:30 a.m. Wednesday in an alley between the 5700 blocks of Kennerly and Maffitt avenues, St. Louis police said. The discovery was made by a girl on her way to school.

The woman, 46, was identified through fingerprints, but authorities were not releasing her name until relatives could be found.

SILENT PAIN

Silent screams of a helpless victim
Make the very essence of my soul shiver.
Silent thoughts of a cold-hearted criminal
Cause my body to quiver.
Silent tears fall down my cheeks
For the life that she led.
Silent images going through my mind
Keep me awake in my bed.

The silence is so loud
It makes my heart want to scream.
Anger and fear consume me.
I don't know what to think,
And there's nothing I can do.
All that is left are the torn remnants
Of a shattered body.

To everyone else,
She is nothing more
Than a newspaper headline
A statistic.

To me?
She is my aunt.
My family.

THE GAMES THAT WE PLAY

With every day that goes by it seems that I understand the world less and less. Trying to figure out where my focus should lie. Recognizing how crucial it is to find joy in the little things.

But do I really try to understand this game called Life? Instead, I seem to focus on a subset of the rules and hope to get by. Still learning how to rejoice in not only the double sixes but also the snake eyes because both mean I get another chance to advance.

With every day that goes by it seems that I understand the world less and less. Should I focus on what makes me happiest to the detriment of my brother, just because that's what society tells me to do? Is this a game of Keep-Away where I do everything that Simon Says?

Maybe I just constantly shift the focus like a Hot Potato in hopes that I never have to say Sorry! Eventually realizing that in not owning up to past mistakes, only one person loses:
Me.

Still with every day that goes by it seems that I understand the world less and less, desperately trying to focus because I'm tired of always playing 52 Card Pickup. Yet in all my confusion, I am able to smile knowing that Someone loves me in spite of myself.

I no longer want to have my Mindtrapped. Playing
Russian Roulette, never knowing what's coming next. So,
I will choose to phone a Friend, and call out to the only
One who can stop this destructive Domino effect.

And yes, that *is* my final answer.

Hide & Seek

See, I thought hide & seek was a game for kids
Reserved for school yards during recess,
But all too often, I regress
To my childhood days
So afraid of being found that I hide,
And stay where it's safe

I can't explain it,
But, there's this fear deep inside of me
Anxiety and pride in me
Masquerading as humility
Got me, shackled
Like, modern-day slavery

And suddenly, it's not a game anymore
My heart exposed
Sin at the core
Still tempted to hide,
Yet, longing for more
And, He's waiting…
Calling me by name
Emancipation has been proclaimed
But, I don't know who I am
Without these chains
'Cause, I've been bound for so long,
It's become the familiar song
And, freedom? – is just some off-key melody,
So I cover my ears and pretend not to hear
That it is for freedom I have been set free
And whom the Son sets free is free indeed,
But, that's just a little too good to be *my* reality

So, I reject the truth and swallow lies
Denying the power of His nail-scarred hands
And the sword in His side
And as I cling to these worthless idols
I forfeit the grace that could be mine
Telling myself that, it'll be different
…next time…

But, I'm tired.
I'm tired of this cycle
They say ignorance is bliss,
But this is straight-up denial
And holding on to this fear
Will lead to the death of me
So I'll forsake the familiar
And say, Lord, come rescue me
Choosing to trust You,
And the depths of Your love for me
No longer held captive,
By the chains of anxiety
And now, I can stop hiding,
I can face myself and the world
And reclaim my true identity
As a child of the King
Who was born
To live free.

Novocaine

It's kinda like…
Novocaine:
A local anesthetic that creates a false reality
Numbing my senses
To the point it convinces
My heart
That it's no longer hurting.
But it never lasts
And what remains is a pain
More intense than
Before I started pretending everything was O.K.
So, like a crack fiend I cling
To the very things that enslave me
Somehow convinced it's the key to being free
Do you see the irony?
Releasing poison in my veins
Instead of Living Water that sustains
As if I didn't realize
As quickly as it came
This high will pass by
It's the very definition of insane
Doing things the same
As if the results will change
But I'm not crazy
Just tired
And longing for relief
But You said if I'd wait for You
You'd renew the strength of the weak
So Jesus, Son of David, have mercy on me
Help me to trust what I know
To believe beyond what I see
Like how You died my death

Just so I could live free
And wouldn't have to try to escape reality
But can face each new day
Safe in Your embrace
Humbled by Your mercy
Captured by Your grace
And now, I must choose
Believe lies that barely pacify
Or trust in You?
It's easier said than done
But I'm tired of this cycle,
So I'll choose to run to instead of from
The only one who can heal and make whole
Has compassion untold
Invites me into freedom
Calls me to be bold
To finally accept my humanity
And lay the anesthetic aside
No longer numb,
But through His death
Made fully alive
I can stop ignoring the pain, fear, and my pride
As I give my life to follow
The One with the nails in His hands,
And the sword in His side
Who by death defeated death
And will one day come again
And gives me hope
That although it's hard right now
This is NOT how my story ends.

ABOUT THE AUTHOR

As a lover of words, Ashley June Smith has been involved in public speaking since the age of nine, and she started writing and performing spoken word poetry as a freshman in high school. Her work has been published in local magazines, and she has been a featured artist at local, regional, and national venues. Ashley is a native of Madison, IL yet has spent much of her time in St. Louis, MO where she was a student at Washington University, and later joined the staff of InterVarsity Christian Fellowship/USA. She currently spends her time helping raise up the next generation of leaders for the Church, community, marketplace, and beyond.